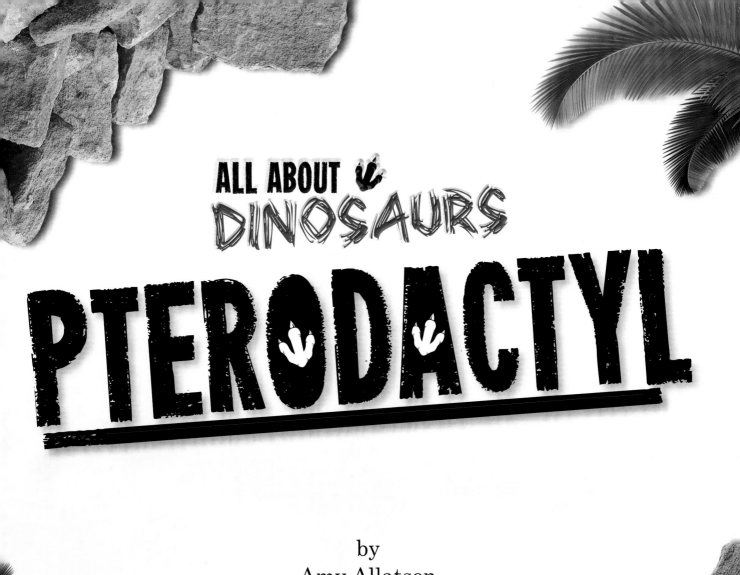

ALL ABOUT DINOSAURS
PTERODACTYL

by
Amy Allatson

KidHaven
PUBLISHING

PHOTO CREDITS

Abbreviations: l-left, r-right, b-bottom, t-top, c-center, m-middle

3 - Suzi44. 4-5 - Catmando. 6-7 - boscorelli. 8m - Philll. 8-9 background - Alexandra Lande. 9m - Valentyna Chukhlyebova. 10 - Michael Rosskothen. 11 - Elenarts. 12 - Elenarts. 13 - andrea crisante. 14 - Paul B. Moore. 15t background - Scandphoto. 15tm - gajdamak. 15m background - Pure Worx. 15m - jhy. 15b background - Chatrawee Wiratgasem. 15bm - Blinka. 16 - Photobank gallery. 17 background - Alexandra Lande. 17m - Catmando. 18-19 background - Iakov Kalinin. 18ml - MarcelClemens. 18br - guysal. 19m - Marques. 20-21m - Valentyna Chukhlyebova. Images are courtesy of Shutterstock.com, with thanks to Getty Images, Thinkstock Photo, and iStockphoto.

Published in 2018 by
KidHaven Publishing, an Imprint of Greenhaven Publishing, LLC
353 3rd Avenue
Suite 255
New York, NY 10010

Designer: Natalie Carr
Editor: Charlie Ogden

Cataloging-in-Publication Data

Names: Allatson, Amy.
Title: Pterodactyl / Amy Allatson.
Description: New York : KidHaven Publishing, 2018. | Series: All about dinosaurs | Includes index.
Identifiers: ISBN 9781534521797 (pbk.) | ISBN 9781534521759 (library bound) | ISBN 9781534521674 (6 pack) | ISBN 9781534521711 (ebook)
Subjects: LCSH: Pterodactyls–Juvenile literature.
Classification: LCC QE862.P7 A45 2018 | DDC 567.918–dc23

Printed in the United States of America

CPSIA compliance information: Batch #BS17KL: For further information contact Greenhaven Publishing LLC, New York, New York at 1-844-317-7404.

Please visit our website, www.greenhavenpublishing.com. For a free color catalog of all our high-quality books, call toll free 1-844-317-7404 or fax 1-844-317-7405.

CONTENTS

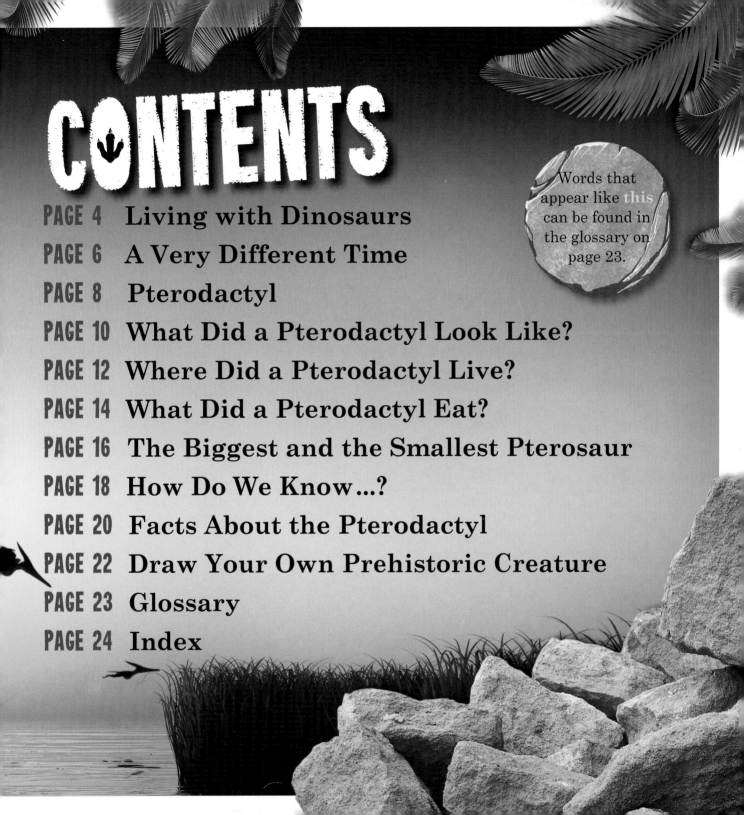

Words that appear like this can be found in the glossary on page 23.

LIVING WITH DINOSAURS

Dinosaurs were **reptiles** that lived on Earth for more than 160 million years before they became **extinct**.

During the time dinosaurs were alive, other creatures shared the earth—and the sky—with them. Pterodactyls were some of these creatures.

A VERY DIFFERENT TIME

Dinosaurs first lived around 230 million years ago during a time called the **Mesozoic** Era. Pterodactyls first appeared on Earth around 150 million years ago.

All land on Earth was together in one piece during the time these creatures lived. Over time, it has slowly split up into different **continents**.

WHEN ALL THE LAND ON EARTH WAS TOGETHER IN ONE PIECE, IT WAS CALLED PANGEA.

PANGEA

PTERODACTYL

NAME	pterodactyl (tehr-uh-DAK-tuhl)
WINGSPAN	up to 3.3 feet (1 m)
WEIGHT	up to 11 pounds (5 kg)
FOOD	carnivore
WHEN IT LIVED	65 million–150 million years ago
HOW IT MOVED	flew and walked on land

Pterodactyls were part of a family of flying reptiles called pterosaurs (TEHR-uh-sohrs). Pterodactyls became extinct around 65 million years ago.

There were many different types of pterosaurs. Pterodactyls were quite small, but other pterosaurs could grow very large.

PTERODACTYL

"PTERODACTYL" MEANS "WINGED FINGER."

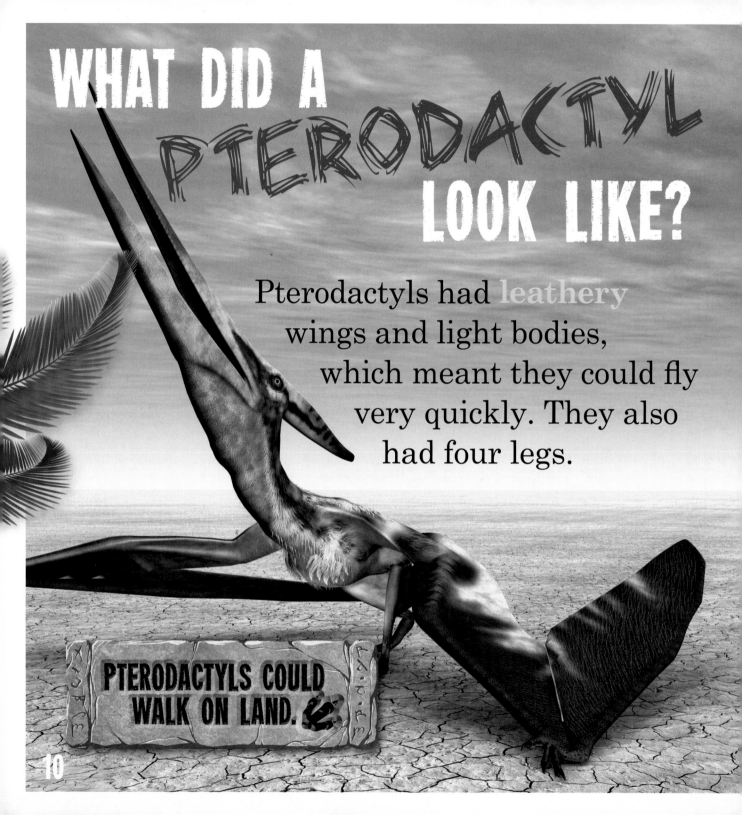

WHAT DID A PTERODACTYL LOOK LIKE?

Pterodactyls had leathery wings and light bodies, which meant they could fly very quickly. They also had four legs.

PTERODACTYLS COULD WALK ON LAND.

CREST

LONG BEAK

Pterodactyls had a long beak for scooping up fish from the water. They also had a long, pointed crest on the back of their head.

WHERE DID A PTERODACTYL LIVE?

Pterodactyls lived in caves and trees, often near water.

Pterodactyls lived in many parts of the world. Their fossils have been found in parts of Europe and Africa.

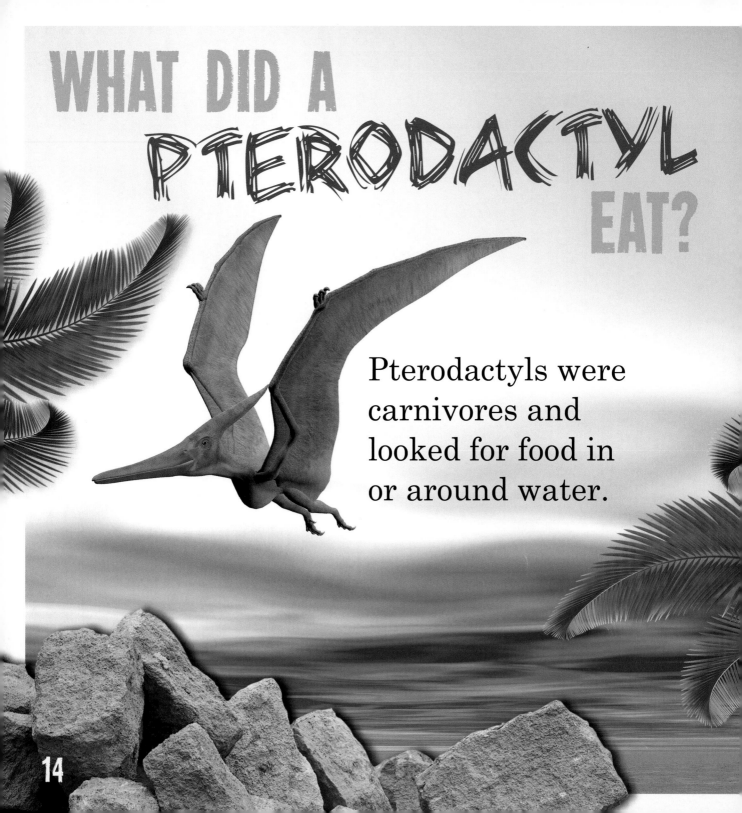

WHAT DID A PTERODACTYL EAT?

Pterodactyls were carnivores and looked for food in or around water.

They ate fish, insects, and other small animals, such as lizards.

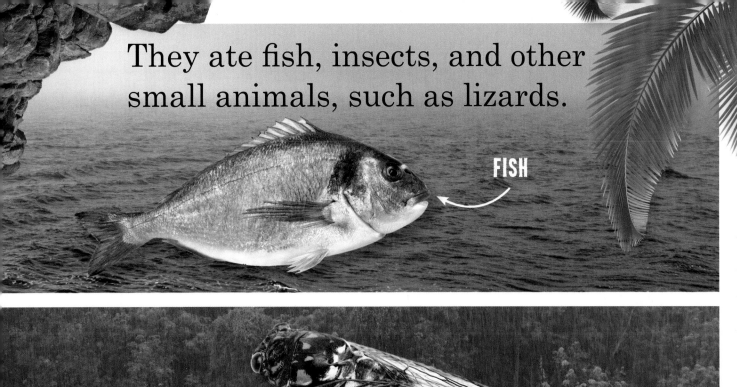

FISH

INSECT

LIZARD

THE BIGGEST AND THE SMALLEST
PTEROSAUR

Some members of the pterosaur family were very big. *Pteranodon* (tuh-RAA-nuh-don) had a wingspan of up to 23 feet (7 m).

PTERANODON'S WINGSPAN WAS THE SAME AS THE HEIGHT OF A FULLY GROWN GIRAFFE!

PTERANODON

However, *Nemicolopterus* (neh-muh-koh-LOP-ter-uhs) was much smaller than *Pteranodon*. It had a wingspan of only 9.8 inches (25 cm).

PTERANODON

NEMICOLOPTERUS

HOW DO WE KNOW...?

We know so much about pterodactyls thanks to the scientists, called paleontologists, who study them. They dig up fossils to find out more about them.

FOSSIL

EGG

18

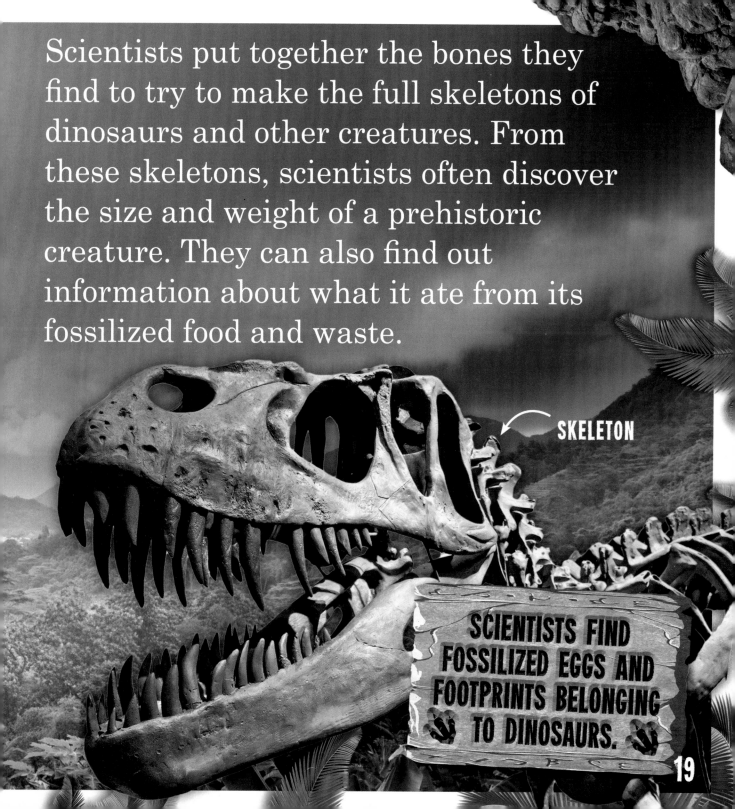

Scientists put together the bones they find to try to make the full skeletons of dinosaurs and other creatures. From these skeletons, scientists often discover the size and weight of a prehistoric creature. They can also find out information about what it ate from its fossilized food and waste.

SKELETON

SCIENTISTS FIND FOSSILIZED EGGS AND FOOTPRINTS BELONGING TO DINOSAURS.

19

FACTS ABOUT THE PTERODACTYL

LEATHERY WINGS

SOME PTERODACTYLS' BEAKS HAD SHARP TEETH.

LONG BEAK

PTERODACTYLS HAD TAILS, BUT THEY WERE VERY SHORT.

UP TO A 3.3 FEET (1 M) WINGSPAN

DRAW YOUR OWN PREHISTORIC CREATURE

THINK ABOUT THESE QUESTIONS ...

1. How does it move?
2. Does it live on land or in water?
3. What does it eat?
4. What color is it?
5. How big is it?

GLOSSARY

carnivore an animal that feeds on other animals

continents any of the seven great masses of land on Earth

extinct no longer alive

fossils the remains of plants and animals that lived a long time ago

leathery like leather, tough

Mesozoic a period of time when dinosaurs lived from 252.2 million years ago to 66 million years ago

reptile a cold-blooded animal with scales

INDEX